# Boston Marriage

*Also by David Mamet*
*available from Methuen*

*Plays*
American Buffalo
The Cryptogram
Dark Pony
Duck Variations
Edmond
Glengarry Glen Ross
Lakeboat
A Life in the Theatre
Mr Happiness
The Old Neighborhood
Oleanna
Reunion
Sexual Perversity in Chicago
The Shawl *and* Prairie du Chien
Speed-the-Plow
Squirrels
The Water Engine
The Woods

*Screenplays*
State and Main

# Boston Marriage

## David Mamet

**Methuen Drama**

Methuen 2001

2 4 6 8 10 9 7 5 3 1

First published in 2001 by
Methuen Publishing Limited
215 Vauxhall Bridge Road, London SW1V 1EJ

Methuen Publishing Limited Reg. No. 3543167

A CIP catalogue record for this book is availabe from the British Library

ISBN 0 413 76600 4

Typeset by SX Composing DTP, Rayleigh, Essex
Printed and bound in Great Britain by
Cox & Wyman Ltd, Reading, Berkshire

# Boston Marriage

*Boston Marriage* was first performed at the American Repertory Theatre, Cambridge, Massachusetts, on 4 June 1999. The cast was as follows:

**Anna**        Felicity Huffman
**Claire**     Rebecca Pidgeon
**Maid**      Mary McCann

*Director* David Mamet
*Set Designers* Sharon Kaitz, J. Michael Griggs
*Costume Designer* Harriet Voyt
*Lighting Designer* John Ambrosone
*Stage Managers* Rosetta E.R. Lee, Tara M. Galvin
*Assistant Director* Robert Milazzo
*Production Associate* Mitchell Sellers

**Characters**

**Anna** *and* **Claire**, *two women of fashion*
*The* **Maid**, *Catherine*

**Scene**

A drawing room.

*Boston Marriage* received its British premiere at the Donmar Warehouse, London, on 8 March 2001. The cast was as follows:

**Anna**        Zoë Wanamaker
**Claire**     Anna Chancellor
**Maid**      Lyndsey Marshal

*Director* Phyllida Lloyd
*Set Designer* Peter McKintosh
*Lighting Designer* Rick Fisher
*Music* Gary Yershon

# Act One

*A drawing room.* **Anna** *is seated in a day dress. She wears a large emerald necklace.* **Claire** *enters.*

**Claire**  I beg your pardon. Have I the right house?

**Anna**  What address did you wish?

**Claire**  Two forty-five.

**Anna**  The number is correct in all particulars.

**Claire**  Then it is the décor which baffles me.

**Anna**  Have you not heard that this one or that, in an idle moment, conceives the idea to redecorate?

**Claire**  Yes.

**Anna**  You have heard?

**Claire**  Indeed. But how does this inspired person pay for it?

**Anna**  He tempers the wind to the shorn lamb.

**Claire**  Who would that be?

**Anna**  It is in the Bible.

**Claire**  And has he an agent on the Earth, GOOD GOD, what is that around your neck?

**Anna**  It is a necklace.

**Claire**  . . . oh, my Lord . . .

**Anna**  What?

**Claire**  Do you not find it . . . somewhat excessive for the morning?

**Anna**  I wear it, should I be summoned on the instant, to choke a horse.

**Claire**  To choke a horse. Are not there men employed precisely for that purpose?

**Anna**  Oh, dear, I should hate to think I was depriving them of livelihood.

**Claire**  How good you are.

**Anna**  Not at all.

**Claire**  Might I be forgiven to ask: Is it Real?

**Anna**  My dear, I have not lost my Taste . . .

**Claire**  Then you have lost your virtue . . . ?

**Anna**  Yes.

**Claire**  Thank God.

**Anna**  A man gave it to me.

**Claire**  A man.

**Anna**  They do have such hopes for the mercantile.

**Claire**  And those hopes so rarely disappointed.

**Anna**  Well, we do love shiny things.

**Claire**  In unity with our sisters the Fish.

**Anna**  Men . . .

**Claire**  What can one do with them?

**Anna**  Just the One Thing.

**Claire**  Though, in your case, it seems to've been effective.

**Anna**  In like a Lion, out like a Lamb. (*Pause.*)

**Claire**  Champion.

**Anna**  Mmm hmm.

**Claire**  This feller fancies you dead rotten.

**Anna**  You don't know the *fraction* of it.

**Claire** Enlighten me.

**Anna** The Jewel.

**Claire** Yes.

**Anna** Not only is it *real:* it is a Family Heirloom.

**Claire** An Heirloom. How better-than-good!

**Anna** Been in his family five generations.

**Claire** Oh finders keepers. Well done!

**Anna** Only conceive, I pray you, that the Jewel is real, my debts are cleared, I have an account at the Dressmaker's, and he has settled upon me, into the bargain, a monthly *stipend* . . .

**Claire** *Stop* . . .

**Anna** I tell you yes. Sufficient to support both me *and* you in Comfort.

**Claire** Oh Bravo. For how glad one is. To see one's friend, come at long last into Safe Harbor.

**Anna** Thank you.

**Claire** Good for you, good for the Side. But . . .

**Anna** Speak.

**Claire** This 'man'.

**Anna** Yes.

**Claire** This, this, this . . .

**Anna** My 'Protector'.

**Claire** Does he not know . . . does he not know your . . . 'reputation'?

**Anna** He is just returned from a long sojourn abroad.

**Claire** What? On the Moon?

**Anna** Ha ha.

**Claire**   Is he in commerce on the Moon?

**Anna**   . . . ha.

**Claire**   Is he a Dealer in Green Cheese? Is that your News? Have you beguiled a Dairy man?

**Anna**   I do not know his profession, or if, indeed, he follows one; I know that he is very rich. That he has been Abroad, and that he, willy-nilly, delights in regaling me with various kickshaws significant of the esteem in which he holds me.

**Claire**   . . . may it continue.

**Anna**   How could it miscarry?

**Claire**   Do not tempt fate.

**Anna**   He worships me. What could go awry?

**Claire**   Has he, for example, a wife?

**Anna**   Why would he require a mistress if he had no wife? Of course he has a wife. But does this 'wife' hold his affection? Does she wear This Jewel, magnificently wrought, unique in all the world?

**Claire**   I must say that it suits you.

**Anna**   I am told some ancestor once staked it against a half province in the Punjab.

**Claire**   At what contest?

**Anna**   . . . could it have been *croquet*?

**Claire**   . . . my golly they played high.

**Anna**   But what *are* riches, whose reflections shine so cold . . .

**Claire**   . . . mmm . . .

**Anna**   . . . in contrast with that true warmth, that sole, true warmth, Of Love and Friendship?

**Claire**    That warmth incalculable and unvarying.

**Anna**    Is it not so?

**Claire**    Which delights in the success of the other.

**Anna**    Aha, aha: I beg your pardon. For do I not perceive in you that roseate glow, my angel, my dove, and words of that character, which must speak of *your* triumph? Yes, I see that you have brought me a bonne bouche to console me for your so cruel and prolonged absence.

**Claire**    You read my story in my face.

**Anna**    When could I not? *How* I have missed you.

**Claire**    One must follow the buffalo herd.

**Anna**    And now you return, with news. You return, not unlike Prometheus. Who brought fire to the gods.

**Claire**    The classical construction, of course, had him steal fire *from* the gods.

**Anna**    He stole fire *from* the gods?

**Claire**    Yes.

**Anna**    And this is generally known?

**Claire**    It is proverbial.

**Anna**    I speak under correction.

**Claire**    Might I have a cup of tea?

**Anna**    Yes, yes, but with no further delay, now *your* news. Inform me.

*The* **Maid** *enters.*

**Maid**    Morning, miss.

**Anna** (*to* **Claire**)    Have you unearthed your *own* protector? Is *that* your report of the World's New Jest? What do you think, Tea, Bridey, eh? Celebratory Tea, and, in fact, we shall have a *party*. That's what we shall do. We shall have . . .

**Claire**   Yes, curiously, that is *not* my news.

**Maid**   It's Catherine, miss.

**Anna**   Yes, we shall have a party, and display through both my ostentation and my taste, the esteem . . .

**Maid**   It's Catherine, miss . . .

**Anna**   . . . excuse me . . . in which I hold you, My Dear Claire. Your place in my heart, and in my home. For what is home without you? A sounding brass or a tinkling cymbal.

**Claire**   That is so well said . . .

**Anna**   It is not mine.

**Claire**   Its employment, however, is so touching.

**Anna**   You spoil me.

**Claire**   I speak but the truth.

**Anna**   We shall have cakes and sweetmeats. The piquant and the sweet. Which only a sense of propriety debars me from conflating with my feelings. For *you*, My et cetera. How I have missed you.

**Claire**   . . . bless you.

**Anna**   Tea, Bridey, do you see? Pen and paper, for we are going to plan a Fête . . .

**Maid**   It's Catherine, miss . . .

**Anna**   And shall we invite, do I see in your eyes, a 'Guest of Honor'? Some Gentleman, perhaps, whom you have 'brought to heel'? Is that your news? Tea, Bridey.

**Claire**   No, that is not my news.

**Maid**   . . . it's Catherine, miss.

**Claire**   I am in Love.

**Anna**    What did you say?

**Maid**    I said it's Catherine . . . (*Pause.*)

**Anna**    Not *Mary*? (*Pause.*) Not 'Mary', I said? Or 'Peggy'?
(*Pause.*) Cringing Irish Terror, is it? What do you want?
Home Rule, and all small children to raise geese? O . . .
Ireland, each and all descended from kings who strode five
miles of lighted streets in Liffey while the English dwelt in
Caves. Is that the general tone, of your Irish divertimento?
(*Pause.*) Eh?

**Maid**    I'm Scottish, miss. (*Pause.*)

**Anna**    Are you? (*Pause.*) I asked you a question.

**Maid**    Yes, miss.

**Anna**    What is the main street in Edinburgh?

**Maid**    I don't know, miss.

**Anna**    Where are you from?

**Maid**    From the Islands.

**Anna**    What islands might those be?

**Maid**    The Orkney Islands, miss.

**Anna**    Where are they situated? (*Pause.*)

**Claire**    Where *are* they?

**Maid**    They're in the water, miss.

**Anna**    What *water* are they in?

**Maid**    . . . what water?

**Anna**    Yes.

**Maid** (*pause*)    In the *sea.*

**Anna**    What's the name of it?

**Maid**    The name of the sea, miss?

**Anna**    Yes. (*Pause.*)

**Maid**   The North Sea, miss.

**Anna** (*pause*)   *Dissolve . . .*

**Maid** *exits.*

**Anna**   Is it the North Sea, then?

**Claire**   I believe it is.

**Anna**   Is it?

**Claire**   I think it is. (*Pause.*)

**Anna**   Is it invariably called that?

**Claire**   I believe so.

**Anna**   Is it the sea we are wont to call the German Sea?

**Claire**   The German Sea.

**Anna**   Is it the same?

**Claire**   I fear that there I disappoint you.

*The* **Maid** *enters. Pause.*

**Anna**   What brings you back?

**Maid**   I've come to clear, miss.

**Anna**   Why would you assume that service required? Has it not been but these two moments you have left the sweetmeats here? Is this some gastronomic monomania of yours? Some distaste for letting food 'sit'? One would have thought to've encountered such in the Southern lands, where heat, engendering maggots, must inspire haste; from which, here in the North, the cold would have been supposed to've offered some protection.

**Claire**   Your mistress suggests you needn't come until she's called you.

**Maid**   She did call me.

**Anna**   To the contrary.

**Maid**    You rang the bell.

**Anna**    Thank you, I haven't rung the bell. I haven't got a bell. D'you see?

**Maid**    I heard a bell.

**Anna**    Well, it is the front door, then. Why don't you answer it?

**Maid** *exits.*

**Anna**    And now, perhaps, to save my worthless life, you'd explain your late announcement. Pray let me but bind myself to the mast.

*The **Maid** passes, in the BG.*

**Anna**    Who is it?

**Maid**    Fella come about the stove.

**Anna**    Yes. What about the stove?

**Maid**    He came to fix it.

**Anna**    Is it broken?

**Maid**    Yes, mum. (*Exits.*)

**Anna**    Oh good. (*Pause.*) How do you find the weather? (*Pause.*) Do you not find it is fine?

**Claire**    I find that it is *seasonable* . . .

**Anna**    . . . yes . . .

**Claire**    . . . for this time of *year.*

**Anna**    Mmm.

**Claire**    And that is as far as I'm prepared to commit myself. (*Pause.*) But I was saying . . .

**Anna**    Yes, you were saying that you were 'in love'. As you phrased it. You were, in midcareer, as it were, prating of this 'Love'.

**Claire**    And you, friend of my Youth . . .

**Anna**    . . . what memory . . .

**Claire**    At the announcement . . .

**Anna**    Yes?

**Claire**    At the announcement, grow if I do not mistake, *cold*. Can you say why?

**Anna**    *Why?*

**Claire**    Yes.

**Anna**    I have redecorated our room in Chintz. In *Chintz*, a fabric I abhor, in your absence, do you see? To please you.

**Claire**    In Chintz?

**Anna**    You once expressed a preference for chintz.

**Claire**    I . . .

**Anna**    For *Chintz*, which I have, oblivious to the verdict of the World, *festooned* . . .

**Claire**    I . . .

**Anna**    I come into funds, I come into funds, and my FIRST THOUGHT, do you see? Is it for myself? It is for *you*. Do I expect thanks? I would be glad of mute appreciation. I receive nothing but the tale of your new rutting. (*Pause.*) Oh how lonely you make me feel. How small. For how can one cherish, nay, how can one respect one, however well formed, who acts so arbitrarily – so cruel? But yes, the engine of the world's betrayal, is it not? And we are sentenced to strive with the world. (*Pause.*)

**Claire**    I'm sorry, what? (*Pause.*) Did I miss anything? (*Pause.*)

**Anna**    I poured out my heart blood.

**Claire**    Oh . . . (*Pause.*) I've forgotten what I was going to say.

**Anna**    Say something *else*. (*Pause.*)

**Claire**    How *practical* you are.

**Anna**    For what *is* speech?

**Claire**    I had often thought, it is as the chirping of the birds, minus their laudable disinterestedness.

**Anna**    Oh what a vast, oh what a vast and pointless shithole it all is.

**Claire**    What would that be?

**Anna**    Our lives.

**Maid** *enters.*

**Anna**    What is it? What do you want? Saving national sovereignty and reparations? What? An apology for your potato famine? IT CAME FROM THE LACK OF ROTATION OF CROPS!!! Do you hear? From a depletion of . . .

**Claire**    Nitrogen.

**Anna**    Nitrogen, or something, in the soil. Do you think that the soil can go on for ever, giving? *Giving.* Never a thought for its replenishment? *Dirt*, do you see? Like every other thing in this green and confusing world, needs conservation and care, no less, in the end, than you and I. It is a thoughtless and, worse, unobservant soul who would say otherwise.

**Maid**    Mum.

**Anna**    But you have my ear.

**Maid**    The dinner, mum.

**Anna**    One would've thought that to've been the province of the cook. (*Pause.*) Oh, no.

**Claire**    You never could keep help.

**Anna**    Did she say it was because of the stove?

**Maid**    She did allow as how she couldn't cook with no stove.

**Claire**    Well, one must credit her argument.

**Anna**    Your attitude smacks of the republican.

**Claire**    You flatter me.

**Anna**    Plead with the cook to stay.

**Maid** *exits.*

**Anna**    But perhaps it is not love.

**Claire**    It is love.

**Anna**    But perhaps it is not.

**Claire**    Then what would it be?

**Anna**    You know, so many of our ills proceed from a corporeal imbalance.

**Claire**    Do they?

**Anna**    I tell you that they do.

**Claire**    How lovely for them. To have, as it were, a provenance. In this gale of uncertainty.

**Anna**    Mmm.

**Claire**    To say, 'I was engendered,' for example, 'by an excess of protein.'

**Anna**    'S were we all, s'far as *that* goes . . .

**Claire**    Ah, yes, your newfound expertise.

**Maid** (*reentering*)    Cook's gone.

**Anna**    Did you not plead with her?

**Maid**    Yes, miss.

**Anna**    What did she say?

**Maid**    She said as how you could kiss her arse. Till . . .

**Anna**   Yes.

**Maid**   She said some holiday, but I've forgot it.

**Claire**   Mayhap it will come to you.

**Maid**   God willing. You know, me Auld Gran used to say . . .

**Anna** (*to the* **Maid**)   Oh, go away. (**Maid** *exits.*) And now we shall have no party; but of course now we have no cause.

**Claire**   Oh, my dear.

**Anna**   Escoffier had it as the last of the pleasures. Which will persist when all the rest have gone.

**Claire**   When all the rest have gone.

**Anna**   Yes.

**Claire**   Escoffier did.

**Anna**   Yes. (*Pause.*)

**Claire**   Is it word one may say in a drawing room?

**Anna**   It is Food.

**Claire** (*pause*)   Food.

**Anna**   Yes.

**Claire**   Food is the pleasure which persists. When all the rest have gone.

**Anna**   According to Escoffier.

**Claire** (*pause*)   And who was he?

**Anna**   A cook.

**Claire**   Well, it would be striking, then, had he said *otherwise.*

**Anna**   Mmm. (*Pause.*) What didja *think* he meant?

**Claire**   Oh, *you* know . . .

**Anna**   Can you not conceive of a Word Above your *Waist?*

**Claire**   And *you*:

**Anna**   Speak:

**Claire**   I come, do you see, I come to you, with my *report* . . .

**Anna**   . . . yes . . .

**Claire**   Of that which I could neither *control* . . .

**Anna**   . . . I take it you are speaking of your loins . . .

**Claire**   Nor . . . ain't *you* an evil old bitch.

**Anna**   I am not old.

**Claire**   Older than I . . .

**Anna**   Hardly true.

**Claire**   What? Have they repealed the *Calendar* . . .

**Anna**   If it were true, it would be cruel to suggest it. You are cruel.

**Claire**   Am I indeed.

**Anna**   Yes. You are.

**Claire**   I have a boon to beg.

**Anna**   Oh what a shithole is the world, and how the friends of youth turn, until time, in its glass, seems to denounce one, and for what enormity? For having glimpsed the light of day too soon. Oh Lord, who seest all, I need a cup of tea. (*Pause.*) Mary. Mary!

**Claire**   I'll tell you what you require. An electric bell.

**Anna**   No. I think I would rather be tied to a canon. I wish that I were dead. (*Pause.*) Why don't you leave? Your errand done, pray, take your congé – you have shattered my heart.

**Claire**   I have to ask a favor.

**Anna**    Well, there is a time for everything. (*Pause.*) Except, of course, those things one has not time for. And what is there to be done about *that*? (*Pause.*)

**Claire**    Can I not induce you to share my . . .

**Anna**    . . . no.

**Claire**    Or, fine, then, to *endorse* . . .

**Anna**    I don't think so.

**Claire**    My happiness.

**Anna**    No. I don't see it happening.

**Claire**    I cannot . . . ?

**Anna**    No. It's just not being done.

**Claire**    Aha.

**Anna**    And why should you require my endorsement? Why, for all that, would you, in the state of, this supposed state of, what?

**Claire**    Bliss.

**Anna**    Require of me anything at all? Would not a traditional understanding of the word 'Bliss' render its meaning 'requiring nothing further of the world'?

**Claire**    Do you know why I particularly hate it when my teeth begin to chatter?

**Anna**    Why is that?

**Claire**    Because they so seldom have anything to say.

**Anna**    Aha. How *bold* it is. How courageous. Rich in that newfound courage. In the light of the New Thing. (*Pause.*) Love? Which, like the Sea, which like religion and expensive jewelry, conquers all. (*Pause.*) Zat the thing?

**Claire**    Yes.

**Anna**    God forgive you.

**Claire**   What am I to do?

**Anna**   . . . *what* is the problem? You told me, but I forgot.

**Claire**   I am in *Love*.

**Anna**   'Love.'

**Claire**   It is a state sung by the poets.

**Anna**   So is death. But I don't see you coming in here beaming and proclaiming, 'I'm dead!'

**Claire**   . . . aha.

**Anna**   'I'm dead! I have *died*! *Embrace* me!' How wonderful for you. Many fine *people* are dead.

**Claire**   How ill your disordered state becomes you.

**Anna**   Tell it to the Marines.

**Claire**   How I preferred my Friend of Old.

**Anna**   Izzat so.

**Claire**   Yes. Full of self-respect, inspiring . . .

**Anna**   And who is the favored one?

**Claire**   . . . awe. Yes, awe, and, more to the point, emulation. In all who beheld her. Her *calm*, her . . .

**Anna**   And what am I to do for a friend?

**Claire**   No, I will always be your friend.

**Anna**   Oh, faugh, you'll . . .

**Claire**   I'll always . . .

**Anna**   . . . until the virus relents, you will be but the most abject boor, fit only to attempt to give or receive sensual satisfaction.

**Claire**   I warrant you that I will always put my, my affection for you . . .

**Anna**   . . . there was a time you would have said 'love' . . .

**Claire**   and my regard for your interests, and your peace of mind . . .

**Anna**   . . . you've ruined my life.

**Claire**   Before everything.

**Anna**   Liar, liar, liar.

**Claire**   Saving, of course,

**Anna**   Say 'equal with'.

**Claire**   . . . I cannot.

**Anna**   Say equal with,

**Claire**   I

**Anna**   . . . those of my beloved.

**Claire**   I

**Anna**   Say it, goddamit to hell.

**Claire**   I cannot.

**Anna**   Say

**Claire**   It is impossible.

**Anna**   Did I say 'mean it'? Did I say 'abjure hypocrisy'? You tell me you have some residual regard for me. I say, that being so, *lie*. You reply that you cannot. Burn in the vile circle of hell reserved for the virtuous and weak.

**Claire**   I

**Anna**   And be damned. Go, and indulge yourself. With the object of your 'love'.

**Claire**   You don't mean it?

**Anna**   Sate yourself, till you are sick of love, then sate yourself with apples, then return to me bloated with roughage, distended . . .

**Claire**   I . . .

**Anna**   *Go* to your, your . . .

**Claire**   . . . I have asked her to come here. (*Pause.*)

**Anna**   You've asked her to come here. Your friend.

**Claire**   Yes.

**Anna**   For, for a vile 'assignation'.

**Claire** (*pause*)   Yes.

**Anna**   And what is your 'boon'? My permission?

**Claire**   I . . .

**Anna**   Have you taken a vow of *arrogance*?

**Claire**   . . . I am in love, I . . .

**Anna**   Yes, so I understood you to have said. It is 'love', you said it was 'love', did you not?

**Claire**   It is love.

**Anna**   And you have, therefore, presumed upon my, my, my, my . . .

**Claire**   Your universally known and lauded generosity.

**Anna**   But what is Love?

**Claire**   . . . what is love?

**Anna**   That we should pine for it.

**Claire**   No, no, I understood that to be your meaning. I require a place. I need a place, at which my friend and I . . .

**Anna**   Your own home being? What? Too Far? Too Cold? Tainted by a life of depravity?

**Claire**   I need a home where I may, with impugnity . . .

**Anna**   . . . mmm?

**Claire**   Take a . . . take a young . . .

**Anna**   How young?

**Claire**    Take a . . .

**Anna**    You Want me to Be Your Beard.

**Claire**    In Short.

**Anna**    You wish me to clothe your nakedness.

**Claire**    I come to you, as I confess myself, as I beseech you, beyond shame.

**Anna**    And this 'shame', this 'shame' you treasure, restores balance to the world, this 'shame', in whose Fine Light, all is permissible.

**Claire**    I have no merit, to plead my case, but her *mother* . . . to whom she is devoted. Do you see? To whom she is, unfortunately, tied. Her *mother* . . .

**Anna**    What about her mother? (*Pause.*)

**Claire**    Well, the young thing cannot travel *unchaperoned*, her mother, who, mistakenly, takes on herself the child's supervision.

**Anna**    How old *is* she?

**Claire**    How old is who?

**Anna**    Your friend. (*Pause.*) I see. And, so having delighted to pollute any residue of your own *reputation*, you make bold to squander mine.

**Claire**    Please.

**Anna**    And you *demean* me by the blithe assumption, that I would consent.

**Claire**    I . . .

**Anna**    That I would Taint, that I would *endanger*, my, my compact with my New Protector . . . Yes. My *Protector*, who provides the very *cushions* upon which we sit. (*Pause.*)

**Claire**    To Market, to Market, to Be a Fat Pig . . .

**Anna**   I did it for *you*, you ill-conditioned sow. I did it for the *cause*. He is a 'man'. What possible joy or diversion for *me* in this arrangement? I did it for *us*, for that unity-of-two which . . .

*Crash in the kitchen.*

**Claire**   Ah, yes. The disruption of the Lowly, mimicking that of the Great.

**Anna**   Perhaps *she's* in love.

**Maid** *enters.*

**Maid**   I'm sorry, mum.

**Anna**   Go away.

**Maid**   I'm sorry, I . . .

**Anna**   Retire.

**Maid**   I dropped the platter.

**Anna**   Go away. Are you deaf? (*Pause.*) Say: are you deaf? From the incessant roaring of the surf upon your savage, native shore? (*Pause.*) Go away. You stink of peat smoke.

**Maid**   We had a coal fire, miss.

**Anna**   And what did you do? *Worship* it? (*Pause.*)

**Maid**   We lit it.

**Anna**   *Did* you?

**Maid**   Yes, mum.

**Anna**   What? To keep you Warm? (*Pause.*) Mmm? In the interminable nights when you lay there, bundled with your livestock, into the one room? Mmm? While the savage and uncaring moon beat down, and so forth, engend'ring dreams of your escape to the Metropolis, thither to torment me? Is that what brings you here? After we've beseeched you to die?

**Maid**   I'm sorry that I dropped the plate, miss.

**Anna**  Ah, yes, *that* was the import of the sound.

**Maid**  You c'n deduct it from my wages.

**Anna**  And live in luxury the rest of my days. Oh good.

**Maid**  And . . . and . . . (*Dissolves in tears.*)

**Claire**  Oh, *now* look what you've done. You never could deal with servants. Let me amend it. (*They watch the* **Maid** *cry for a while.*) What is it? You're with child, by the man who pledged to marry you, now you discovered he's a wife and babe at home? (*Pause.*) Zat it? Something like that? (*Pause.*) Mmm? You try . . .

**Anna**  Y'r Da is dying of the Black Lung from a life spent in the Collieries, 'n' you lack the four pence which could transport him to rest and renewed vigor? (*Pause.*) Which is it? (*Pause.*) *Choose.* (*The* **Maid** *exits.*) And now the tea will remain cold. (*Pause.*) Quite cold. 'N' who have I to blame. But myself. And an impersonal, and thoughtless deity. (*Pause.*)

**Claire**  Help me.

**Anna**  You are without shame.

**Claire**  I have confessed it.

**Anna**  Ah, no love as foolish as an Old Woman's love. (*Pause.*) An Old Woman's love. A HAG, et cetera, shorn of all, save those last vestiges of beauty, those final shreds, not clothing, nay, but Framing her horrible plain face and form, that crone, reduced to sophistry to lure the young and the beautiful into her sway. And this is what it comes to, at the cold-fag end. To sit in dead conversation with the Duenna, to offer 'cookies' to the chaperone, while you, and your young . . . no, the mind cannot compass it. Oh what a constantly disrupted . . . Oh what a disorderly . . . Oh what a sad thing. The endless capacity of the world to unseat and disappoint us. Do you believe in God?

**Claire**  I would if you'd shut up.

**Anna**   And do you begrudge me my 'keening'?

**Claire**   Oh, pull your socks up.

**Anna**   . . . I . . .

**Claire**   Every note you strike is false. I cannot assemble them into a rational composition. You're like a piano so bad out of tune that the choice of any note is arbitrary. How can one respect you? (*Pause.*)

**Anna**   I beg your pardon.

**Claire**   And I am sorry I was moved to speak with enthusiasm.

**Anna**   I have forgotten it.

**Claire**   You are too kind to live.

**Anna** (*pause*)   Sherry?

**Claire**   Perhaps just a touch.

**Anna**   . . . and you would have this young Person come to my home.

**Claire**   Yes.

**Anna**   When?

**Claire**   Today.

**Anna**   You presume much. Yes – even now, I see you scour the street. This is the new thing, then. This is that for which it has amused God to spare me. (*Pause.*) Fine.

**Claire**   . . . I beg your pardon?

**Anna**   Have her come. (*Pause.*)

**Claire**   You don't mean it.

**Anna**   I shall grant graciously what I dare not refuse.

**Claire**   Bless you, Oh Best of Friends.

**Anna**   Is it not so?

**Claire**    It *is* so. It *is* so.

**Anna**    Godspeed you, and your Young Friend, to your Hour of Bliss.

**Claire**    And God preserve you . . .

**Anna**    Joy to your sheets.

**Claire**    And may heaven both witness and endorse your sainted humanity.

**Anna**    . . . please . . . (*They drink.*) But may I, whilst preserving that essential veil of 'decency' . . .    *– Cautious*

**Claire**    Yes.    *dip head + eye contact*

**Anna**    Inquire . . .    *– drawling*

**Claire**    . . . please?

**Anna** (*pause*)    That is, you take my meaning, 'Does' she, or . . . to put it differently, 'have' you . . . (*Pause.*)    *– Cautious*

**Claire**    She does not. We have not.

**Anna**    Yes. Then, I have my own request.    *– Happy*

**Claire**    Anything under heaven.

**Anna**    To, let us say, to, to *participate*, in . . .

**Claire**    I fear that my *vision* of the meeting . . .

**Anna**    Yes.

**Claire**    Of the 'geometry' of the thing . . .

**Anna**    Quite, no, you mistake me. I only meant to the extent that I . . . set the *scene*, *ease* the transition, as it were: I, I bring you *cocoa*, I open the windows, and suggest you two would be more 'cozy', underneath a 'throw', I . . .

**Claire**    Yes, thank you, but . . .

**Anna**    Do you see? In the capacity of a *stage* manager, or . . .

**Claire**   I . . .

**Anna**   Yes, this shall be our party. And we must have a pie. Stress cannot exist in the presence of a pie.

**Claire**   A pie.

**Anna**   It casts out stress as the heat of the hand repels quicksilver. Faugh I say. Faugh. Keep you your precious vapors, your fantods, your anxiety. Give me a pie. Give me a pie *anyday*.

**Claire**   Give me a pie, too. But . . .

**Anna**   For there is that of the bucolic in it. Is there not? The pie, the cottage, the . . .

**Claire**   The *hearth*, finally.

**Anna**   Little Nell. Nell or Molly.

**Claire**   Young . . .

**Anna**   That's right.

**Claire**   Young Susan. Her brown arms shapely from the work of the field. One wisp of her . . .

**Anna**   Dark blond hair.

**Claire**   If you will, come down on her eyes. Brushed back with the flour-covered forearm. As she *kneads* the dough we may see the tendons now assemble now disperse beneath the nut-brown skin. She looks up: 'I'm making a pie.' (*Pause.*)

**Anna**   Do you mock me?

**Claire**   I am concocting a seduction. I do not require a pâtissière. (*Pause.*)

**Anna**   What is there risible about a pie?

**Claire**   Fine. And we must have ices.

**Anna**   'Ices.'

**Claire**   I believe so. (*Pause.*)

**Anna**    Ices.

**Claire**    Yes.

**Anna**    . . . at a seduction?

**Claire**    And what, party favors, little, what are they? One gives them to the Cook.

**Anna**    Wallets.

**Claire**    That's right. And the odd vial of scent.

**Anna**    I just said 'a pie'.

**Claire**    I riposted ices.

**Anna**    . . . but . . .

**Claire**    What is it you find abhorrent in them? Is it their, their artificial *color*, mmm? Or their *Frigidity* . . . (*Pause.*)

**Anna**    Oh. (*Pause.*)

**Claire**    I beg you to accept my deep and unreserved apology, my tongue has run away with me. I have traduced both the memory of our friendship and the fact of our love. I am alone, in the midst of my own folly, of my need and vice. I stand naked before you, in my panting and unclean depravity, and beg for your aid. *Help* me.

**Anna** (*pause*)    All right.

**Claire**    Oh, Blessed forgiveness.

**Anna**    But I want to watch.

**Claire**    You whore.

**Anna**    Not in the room. Not in the *Room*. What do you take me for, my God.

**Claire**    You Pagan slut.

**Anna**    Through a *hole* in the wall.

**Claire**    No.

**Anna**   Did I say I want to *participate*? Or *Comment*?

**Claire**   I said no.

**Anna**   Or *advise*, which, given the *youth* of the . . .

**Claire**   I said no.

**Anna**   . . . might *not* be beside the point.

**Claire**   Rave on.

**Anna**   Ah. Yes. Love. Love for thee, but not for *me*. *My* sacrifice is *naught*. While *you*, yes . . . *Gaze* through the window. Gaze in vain, while we may sit here and beguile the hour, in parsing the distinction between Friendship and Acquaintance. Lug your trick off to the park. Amuse the *nannies* with their *prams*. 'What's that, nanny?' 'Well, that's just two women, dear.' 'But, nanny, what are they *doing*?' Off you go.

**Claire** (*at the window*)   Oh my God. It is she. I recognize the barouche.

**Anna**   Oh, your new friend. Is she come?

**Claire**   She is here.

**Anna**   Hard cheese.

**Claire**   Oh, what is more foolish than the unrequited love of the old? (*Pause.*) I beg you . . .

**Anna**   Ah.

**Claire**   . . . if . . .

**Anna**   No, no, it is not enough, my dear, to say, 'I see the Penalty, pray do not tax yourself inflicting it.'

**Claire**   I beg your pardon. It is a sign of my distraction . . . I plead with you: anything within my power. I'd do it for you, you know I would. Were the situation reversed.

**Anna**   But the situation, you will allow, is *not* reversed.

**Claire**   Cold, heartless woman.

**Anna**   Am I, indeed?

**Claire**   Of whom they once said heart of bronze if any heart at all.

**Anna**   Izzat what they once said?

**Claire**   Once, yes, once we strove together.

**Anna**   I do seem to remember.

**Claire**   A small band of Freebooters, share alike . . .

**Anna**   . . . yes, it was so . . .

**Claire**   And now, as you've come into your Patrimony . . .

**Anna**   Aha . . .

**Claire**   You've found a *Protector*. And the Emerald Round your Neck the ensign of that selfishness, that Jealousy Engendered by Wealth . . .

**Anna**   Aha.

**Claire**   For it's riches that have sundered you.

**Anna**   Is it indeed?

**Claire**   You say Share Alike, and *I* say: your abode, for Part of One Day . . .

**Anna**   Yes, it is not exactly the 'use of the Hall', which . . .

**Claire**   Cold, cold, ancient, jealous hag.

**Anna**   I see you are disordered. Shall I loosen your stays?

**Maid** (*entering*)   There's a young person at the door.

**Anna**   Yes. No, I'm not at all sure that I am 'at home'. Oh my. No, I am not at home. Pray, have her call again some other time.

**Claire**   Yes. You shall set the scene. You shall set the scene and aid me, aid the two of us by the tone, by, by the gracious attentions . . .

**Anna**   . . . that is all I asked.

**Claire**   It shall be as you say.

**Anna**   Then we may proceed. (*Exits.*)

**Maid**   Lovely day for it, miss. But I'd wear my hat.

**Claire**   I *beg* your pardon.

**Maid**   ''F I went for a walk.

**Claire**   Ah, yes, I mistook you.

**Maid**   What'd you *think* I meant?

**Claire**   Nothing.

**Maid**   I wouldn't wear me hat in *bed* . . .

**Claire**   . . . what reserve.

**Maid**   'Cause, then, it, maybe, would get *crinkled*.

**Anna** *reenters.*

**Anna**   Yes, it seems it is your young friend. I must endorse and second your choice. Charming.

**Claire**   And you will afford us privacy and shelter. For the Afternoon.

**Anna**   And participate,

**Claire**   within the limits of . . .

**Anna**   . . . as agreed.

**Claire**   And you swear to divert her chaperone?

**Anna**   She has come alone.

**Claire**   Oh, Joy.

**Anna**   And we are agreed as to terms?

**Claire**   We are. Urge her in.

**Claire** *nods.* **Anna** *walks to the doorway and addresses a person, off.*

**Maid** (*off*)    Miss, I didn't catch yer name?

**Anna** (*off*)    Welcome, yes, Welcome to my Abode. How *good* of you to come, if you would be so kind as to, Bridey. Bridey. Would you please . . .

**Claire**    If you'd excuse me . . . (*Brushes past them.*)

**Maid**    It's Catherine, miss.

**Anna**    Good lookin' little thing, eh?

**Maid**    I couldn't say, miss.

**Anna**    No, indeed, she is. And you yourself, you know, you are not unattractive.

**Maid**    What, mum?

**Anna**    Has no one told you that before?

**Maid**    No, mum.

**Anna**    Aha. Do you garner the thrust of my declaration?

**Maid**    I think so, mum.

**Anna**    But what, it repels you?

**Maid**    No, mum, but.

**Anna**    Yes?

**Maid**    What would I tell me parents?

**Anna**    That you had found a secure position.

**Maid**    May I think about it?

**Anna**    Indeed.

**Maid**    Thank you, mum.

**Claire** *reenters.*

**Claire**    She is upset.

**Anna**  Well, La! How that astonishes me. One must set the stage. Proceed with measure. And you will thank God that I am here to pace your advances.

**Claire**  It is not my advances which upset her.

**Anna**  Say, then.

**Claire**  She asks me about *you*.

**Anna**  About me – She is *jealous*. She is *jealous*, the dear thing.

**Claire**  She is not jealous.

**Anna**  Is she not, then what is it about me upsets her?

**Claire**  She asks why you are wearing her mother's necklace.

# *Act Two*

## Scene One

*The drawing room.* **Anna** *is seated alone. Catherine, the* **Maid**, *enters.*

**Anna**   Someone was at the door?

**Maid**   Yes, miss.

**Anna**   What was the message?

**Maid**   Message?

**Anna**   Do not spare me. I am prepared.

**Maid**   There wuunt no message.

**Anna**   Then who was at the door?

**Maid**   It was the fella 'bout the stove. He said . . .

**Anna**   Has no one left a letter?

**Maid**   No, miss.

**Anna**   Fell circumstance. Oh, how you chastise my presumption. I am undone. My protector will withdraw his stipend as my love, her love, and I shall starve, the hollow percussion of my purse, a descant to that of my broken heart. But once I was young and the world before me. And once men were other than the depraved swine time and experience have revealed them to be. Once the world was to me a magic place . . . I was a Little Girl, Oh, once . . .

**Maid**   D'you mind if I work while you're talkin', miss? (*Pause.*) 'Ld it disturb you, like? You needn't think, like, that I'd evade yer privacy. (*Pause.*) Cause I can't, the life o'me, tell what the fuck yer on about. (*Pause.*)

**Anna**   I was speaking of my shattered dreams.

**Maid**   Don't let me hinder ye.

**Anna**    Most kind.

**Maid**    Because me Auld Gran used to say . . .

**Anna**    Will you, for the love of God, shut up?

**Maid**    Yes, mum . . .

**Anna**    Has no one called?

**Maid**    Not to the best of my knowledge, no. (*Pause.*)

**Anna**    Ah, then, good-bye to Comfort . . .

**Maid**    . . . Fella said that I bring it on myself.

**Anna**    . . . good-bye to joy, and good-bye to my own lover for whom I strove to 'feather our nest' . . . That you bring what on yourself?

**Maid**    Criticism.

**Anna**    I have no doubt that you do.

**Maid**    B'cause . . .

**Anna**    In fact, I've seen it demonstrated.

**Maid**    Because . . . (*Dissolves crying.*)

**Anna**    *What?* (*Pause.*) What? Are you crying?

**Maid**    No, miss.

**Anna**    Have you no *sympathy*, I have lost my income, and I've alienated the affection of my one true love. What is your particular complaint? (**Maid** *sobs.*) Oh fine, fine. Go on. Heave your apron to your eyes.

**Maid**    It's too short, miss.

**Anna**    Well, then, run in and *change.* (*Pause.*) Put on a longer apron.

**Maid**    They're in the wash.

**Anna**    Well, you should have thought ahead. (**Maid** *cries.*) *What . . . ?*

**Maid**   Miss, I'm that homesick, I swear, that I'd fuck the ragman just to hear a friendly word.

**Anna**   Believe me, I know the feeling.

**Maid**   I'm sure you do.

**Anna**   What *can* you mean . . . ? (*Doorbell rings.*) Go. Get the door. I am prepared.

**Maid** *exits.* **Claire** *enters.*

**Claire**   What have you heard?

**Anna**   Oh, thank God, you are returned.

**Claire**   What have you heard?

**Anna**   Thank God. I feared that I had alienated you.

**Claire**   She has not . . . ? She has not written.

**Anna**   She . . .

**Claire**   My young friend.

**Anna**   Oh.

**Claire**   Has she?

**Anna**   What could she write?

**Claire**   She could write her love, could she not? Or she could write, oh God, she could write that we, though momentarily thwarted . . .

**Anna**   I would say, my dear, that the communiqué which we have to *fear* is from her fff –

**Claire**   From her father.

**Anna**   Wouldn't you say?

**Claire**   From her *father*?

**Anna**   He has been discovered in a malversation, do you see, of his wife's jewelry. And how was it discovered? His daughter came to a depraved and illicit assignation and

spied it draped round the neck of her intended's tribad
paramour.

**Claire**    Have you taken up Journalism?

**Anna**    What a vile thing to say.

**Claire**    You look like a dead cart horse.

**Anna**    . . . is that my muff?

**Claire**    You gave it to me *years* ago. How Dare You . . . do
you stoop to, to, to, to *attempt* to humble me, by calling up
past favors?

**Anna**    No.

**Claire**    Then what was the import of your mention of the
muff?

**Anna**    I was surprised it had come back in style.

**Claire**    God damn you to hell.

**Anna**    I suppose if one waits long enough . . .

**Claire**    You look like a plate of cold stew.

**Anna**    I did not sleep last night.

**Claire**    And I shall never sleep again. I shall stand vigil,
my Burning eyes fixed on eternity, awaiting that word which
will never come.

**Anna**    They *will* call, of course.

**Claire**    Oh, do you think, Oh Good!

**Anna**    They will call to demand the return of the
necklace . . .

**Claire**    To demand the necklace.

**Anna**    For a certainty.

**Claire**    Aha.

**Anna**    I have it here. (*She takes out a small jewelry bag.*)

**Claire**    How come you to act so Blithe?

**Anna**    Why care I for the loss of a Jewel? Let him restore it, to his 'wife', or . . . *whatever* employee of his he has filched it from.

**Claire**    And take with him, will he not, all your support, your equipage, your . . .

**Anna**    That must be as it will be.

**Claire**    Do you not find such a disposition trivial?

**Anna**    It is, as I understand the term, *Philosophy.* (*Pause.*) How can philosophy be trivial? When you have known me to be trivial?

**Claire**    You once referred to the Crimean War as 'just one of those Things'.

**Anna**    I did?

**Claire**    Yes.

**Anna**    When did I do that?

**Claire**    During a discussion of Geopolitics.

**Anna**    What is or are Geopolitics?

**Claire**    Oh, *you* remember . . .

**Anna**    I do not.

**Claire**    They are, as the term might suggest, the politics of the world.

**Anna**    And why were we discussing them?

**Claire**    To pass the time. To pass the time, you vacant cow. That is what people do. When they are thrust together. During *dinner*, or . . .

**Anna**    Yes . . .

**Claire**    Or, *marriage* . . .

**Anna**    Yes, you do fight shy of the domestic.

**Claire**    *Do* I?

**Anna**    I must say you do.

**Claire**    Why would *that* be?

**Anna**    It baffles me.

**Claire**    Does it, indeed?

**Anna**    Yes. Which situation has So Much to Offer.

**Claire**    To 'those of that bent'.

*Doorbell rings. Pause. Rings again.* **Maid** *enters.*

**Maid**    I'm goin' to get the door. (*Pause.* **Maid** *exits.*)

**Anna**    Are you prepared?

**Claire**    I am prepared.

**Anna**    Oh, fate inexorable. Oh, fate misthought at first to be but circumstance, revealed at last as the minute operations of the gods. Oh fate but our own character congealed into a burning glass. Focus your cleansing light upon me, and I shall be cleansed.

**Claire** (*mumbling*)    . . . you *gave* me this goddamned muff . . .

**Maid** *enters.*

**Anna**    Show them in.

**Maid**    Show who in? (*Pause.*)

**Anna**    Who was at the door?

**Maid**    It was the Stove Mechanic. He said . . .

**Anna**    I don't care what he said.

**Claire**    Why has he come again, if the stove is operational?

**Maid**    It ain't exactly operational.

**Claire**    In what respects is it deficient?

**Maid**   You need some new parts. He . . .

**Anna**   Go away.

**Maid**   He . . .

**Anna**   You are unwanted. And the tea is cold.

**Maid**   . . . nothing the matter with cold tea . . .

**Anna**   . . . I beg your pardon?

**Maid**   I've had worse, and so, I'd think, have you. No offense.

**Anna**   'No offense'? You impertinent *cooze* . . .

**Maid**   I only meant, in a long life, some point, it's likely come down to Short Rations. (*Pause.*)

**Anna**   In a long life.

**Maid**   Yes, miss. (*Exits.*)

**Anna**   Oh, how the Lesser Beasts draw strength, at the spectacle of the Lioness beset.

**Claire**   . . . oh, God.

**Anna**   And All is Confusion, at the Waterhole.

**Maid** (*reentering*)   Mum.

**Anna**   Go away, or I'm going to have you killed.

**Claire**   How would you go about it?

**Anna**   Well, I'm sure there are ways.

**Claire**   You are?

**Anna**   Of course. One reads of it all the time.

**Claire**   Mmm?

**Anna**   In the Papers? 'Such and so, having engaged the services of an Assassin . . .'

**Claire**   Isn't that 'having left my Bed and Board . . .'

**Anna**   You think with your loins.

**Claire**   Oh, Land of Goshen. Oh, how more than droll. What of your Bible now? What of Forbearance, meek and mild . . .

**Anna**   . . . kiss my ass.

**Claire**   Ho, but perhaps they'll come again. Perhaps my Love, and perhaps your Protector. Blind to your past, indifferent to your limitations, rich as Croesus. Perhaps they approach now. Yes, as all things can be mended by wishing; as the child, mangled by the cart, can be made whole by apology. You have fucked my life into a cocked hat. (*She begins to cry.* **Anna** *goes to her to comfort her.*)

**Anna**   There, there . . .

**Claire**   Oh, thank you, I feel so much better.

**Claire**   We shall end life together, old and friendless, desired by no one, devoid of all save memory, and these most wistful of words:

**Maid** (*entering*)   While I was lookin' at your muff, your parts came. (*Pause.*)

**Claire**   I beg your pardon.

**Maid**   I was admiring your muff.

**Claire**   It was a gift from a friend.

**Maid**   And while I was distracted, mum, yer parts came.

**Anna**   My parts?

**Maid**   The parts for the stove.

**Anna**   Thank you, that will be all. (**Maid** *exits. To* **Claire**.) Now, listen and be taught.

**Claire**   No.

**Anna**   I say Yes. I offer you the comforts of philosophy. Your little friend, your young friend, she was just a passing whim.

**Claire**   And he was your last chance.

**Anna**   Yes, that is cruel, but I forgive you. Shall I tell you why? As neither you nor I is perfect. *Both* of us have gone astray.

**Claire**   You make me throw up.

**Anna**   We've gone astray. We have become habituated to that vile weed, Luxury, which grows, in the night, like the *Ricinus* plant, in the Bible.

**Claire**   The plant in the Bible.

**Anna**   Yes.

**Claire**   In the Morning Room?

**Anna**   I beg your pardon?

**Claire**   The one near the Ficus? Do you know, and here again, I always *told* you. You listen to nothing, My dear. You have a diverting and quixotic *view* of things, but you take advice from nothing that lives.

**Anna**   What do you mean?

**Claire**   I told you repeatedly it was too damp in there.

**Anna**   In where?

**Claire**   In the morning room.

**Anna**   You never said anything remotely of the sort.

**Claire**   I ruined a perfectly good, what do you mean I never said anything? I ruined my new black velvet *reticule*.

**Anna**   . . . if . . .

**Claire**   I, *excuse* me. In This House of Horrors. *That* night, we, but I see you have repressed it.

**Anna**   . . . repressed *what?* . . .

**Claire**   . . . and how *dare* you take refuge in the Bible?

**Anna**   . . . many recur to it in times of Stress.

**Claire**   . . . what nonsense.

**Anna**   Quite the contrary.

**Claire**   You have ruined my life.

**Anna**   Things Occur. Claire. I *pray* you, do not mope, and fret. Things occur. That is their nature. Do you see? Change . . .

**Claire**   Change.

**Anna**   It is the nature of all things.

**Claire**   *'Change . . .'?*

**Anna**   Yes.

**Claire**   Oh, how I loathe a poseur.

**Anna**   Please?

**Claire**   You mean to denigrate my loss, by your display of equanimity in the face of your own.

**Anna**   *Have* I not undergone, you will forgive my ironic employment of the term 'a reversal'?

**Claire**   And what of my reticule?

**Anna**   Bother your reticule. (*Pause.*) What reticule?

**Claire**   . . . we had met at a certain person's house, I see it clear as Arctic day, and you perceived such and such a one was forming, an attachment for me. And I repaired here, after the fête, with, as I then thought, the best of boon companions, whereupon you jealously began to *sulk*. And I had laid my reticule upon the étagère, in the solarium, next to your dread ficus plant, which dripped upon my reticule and left it water-spotted and ruint. Then . . .

**Anna**    I stipulate to the tale's essential verity.

**Claire**    . . . you remember it?

**Anna**    No, but I'd swear to heresies untold if you'd shut up. What is your point?

**Claire**    That I'd informed you, at that time, that you maintained an overdank and fetid atmosphere in the solarium. It dropped on my reticule. And now it's rotted your Bible.

**Anna**    Oh. Ha. Oh, ha. Oh ha ha ha ha ha.

**Claire**    You have the advantage of me.

**Anna**    It grows in the story of Jonah.

**Claire**    What?

**Anna**    The *Ricinus* plant.

**Claire**    Of Jonah and the Whale.

**Anna**    Yes. In the Bible.

**Claire**    A plant.

**Anna**    Yes. You unlettered spiv.

**Claire**    Which has what reference for us?

**Anna**    I *opined* . . .

**Claire**    Yes . . .

**Anna**    That I had grown inured to luxury. Until the increasing need of it, do you see?

**Claire**    . . . I am too ill for words.

**Anna**    . . . where is your sense of humor?

**Claire**    Where *is yours*?

**Anna**    Oh la. Where could it be?

**Claire**    Gone to Arcturus, with the rest of the light . . .

**Anna**   Where *is* Arcturus?

**Claire**   In the Heavens.

**Anna**   Is it a star?

**Claire**   I would think so.

**Anna**   Far far away?

**Claire**   Of necessity.

**Anna**   Lover's agog at the 'immensity' of it all.

**Claire**   . . . yes?

**Anna**   Good then, see here, the star. It's not *yours*. Do you know? It's not your soul. It's the sky. It sits there and displays this or that trick of the light, and your kidneys, or spleen, direct you to mate, and you gaze upward.

**Claire**   Mmm.

**Anna**   Because you are a *poet?* No. BECAUSE YOU ARE OUTSIDE. It would seem equally sublime, were you cased in a *piano* crate, squinting at the screws.

**Claire**   . . . indeed.

**Anna**   It is none other than our friend, the Mating Instinct.

**Claire**   Mmm.

**Anna**   Toying with you. Once again.

**Claire**   And what would you know of that? Greek to a Goose.

**Anna**   I pray you would indulge me for a space, for I am going to set out on a speech, which may have some duration, but whose theme may be inferred from its opening phrase: HOW DARE YOU?

**Claire**   No. No. No. It is not *fair*. Do you see? It is not *fair*.

**Anna**   What is 'fair'? Is Love Fair?

**Claire**   Mmm.

**Anna**   Is it fair, that the sea, for example, should rage wide and savage, erasing whole towns and coastal . . .

**Claire**   Settlements?

**Anna**   No, well, yes, certainly, but I meant the . . . the . . . the sites of agriculture . . . (*Pause.*)

**Claire**   'Farms'?

**Anna**   Thank you. Then retreat to that calm beauty so cherished by painters of the second class? (*Pause.*)

**Maid** *enters.*

**Anna**   Have they come? Have they called? What is it? Has a letter arrived?

**Maid**   No, miss.

**Anna**   Well then, what brings you here? Sick Curiosity? Come for the Spectacle . . . ? Oh, no. I see it: Years to come: our Martha here, back in Ireland, reinstalled by her Peat fire, the wee bairns, listening, once again, to grandmother's saga, 'My time in the City', listening, each for her favorite part, for one the splendor, for one the *scope* . . .

**Claire**   . . . for one the end.

**Anna**   In the so-heavy odor of the village bodies, in that 'hut', where the very caulking, of the walls . . . What is it made of? What is it made of? The, the caulking . . .

**Claire**   What's it made of?

**Maid**   Mud.

**Anna**   'Miss.'

**Maid**   Mud, miss.

**Claire**   Of that river mud, so suggestive of sex to the pre-orgasmic mind, that mud . . .

**Maid**   Actually, they dig it from the barrow, miss.

**Claire**   From the barrow.

**Maid**   From the Hill. Me Auld Gran used to say . . .

**Claire**   I know what a barrow is.

**Maid**   Yes, miss.

**Claire**   I *wondered* that the *Barrow* mud was *moist* enough. (*Pause.*) Of fog, sweat, peat smoke, and that ineffable *reek* so redolent of . . . *childbirth*, menstrual blood, of copulation, of . . .

**Maid**   Actually, it isn't moist, miss. That's why it falls out. (*Pause.*) It dries up.

**Claire**   It dries up.

**Maid**   The mud. (*Pause.*)

**Claire**   What do they do then?

**Maid**   They, well. They moisten it, and they replace it.

**Anna**   Whyn't they just use moister mud?

**Maid**   Well, I'm sure that they do, you see, but, but, but, but, that, as time goes by . . .

**Anna**   Mmm hmm.

**Maid**   . . . it all dries out. (*Pause.*)

**Claire**   Aha.

**Maid**   However you moisten it. (*Starts to cry.*)

**Anna**   Why are you crying?

**Maid**   Cause I'll have to leave.

**Anna**   Have you been spying on your Betters?

**Maid**   What, miss?

**Claire**   Eavesdropper.

**Anna**   Is that the happy excuse for your visit? To profess your chagrin over our reversal?

**Maid**   Yes, that's right, miss. I came to see was there 'Nything I c'ld do to *help*.

**Claire**   Oh, Wizard! Brave Sorority indomitable. Come to support us in our grief. Yes. Boil Water. Make a poultice. (*Pause.*)

**Anna**   What?

**Claire**   What could you do to help?

**Maid**   I was goin' to say, that It's like *rowing*.

**Anna** (*pause*)   What is like rowing?

**Maid**   The troubles between women and men.

**Claire**   Pray. How is it like rowing?

**Maid**   Men have big shoulder blades. Our shoulder blades are smaller. Which means less power rowing. Although, if you row *correctly*, you should use yer *legs*, which, women, have big muscles in our *legs*. (*Pause.*) Though, of course, it don't make much difference in a *short* pull. (*Pause.*)

**Anna**   What doesn't make a difference?

**Maid**   Rowing.

**Claire**   Why does it make that much difference, then, rowing a long way?

**Maid**   Because, miss, like many things in life, a lack of form can be hid in the short run, its absence being taken up by *power*. (*Pause.*)

**Claire**   How do you come to know so much about the nautical?

**Maid**   I was on a boat once.

**Claire**   *Really.*

**Anna**   That will be all. (**Maid** *exits. Pause.*)

**Claire**   You were going to say something.

**Anna**    What about?

**Claire**    How the deuce should *I* know . . . ? (*Pause.*)

**Anna**    I've forgotten what I was going to say.

**Claire**    Your mind is a very sieve.

**Maid** *enters.*

**Maid**    Mum.

**Anna**    Oh MIGHT YOU GET OFF MY TITS? What *is* it? (*Pause.*)

**Maid**    I've told a lie.

**Claire**    Well, then you're going to hell.

**Anna**    A lie about what?

**Maid**    I can't rightly say it.

**Anna**    Oh, spit it out.

**Maid**    It's me's in trouble.

**Anna**    Go on.

**Maid**    I've lost me most precious possession.

**Claire**    Your Rapier Wit?

**Maid**    No.

**Claire**    I give up. (*Pause.*)

**Maid**    Me *maidenhood.*

**Claire**    How icky.

**Anna**    When did it occur?

**Maid**    During before when you had your tea.

**Anna**    Aha.

**Maid**    No, not the *whole* of it.

**Anna**    No.

**Maid**   . . . jus' between the first time that you rang for the Hot water.

**Anna**   Mmm.

**Maid**   No, not even. No, I tell a lie. It was when I came back with the tray.

**Anna**   Yes . . .

**Maid**   But b'fore I put the tray down.

**Anna**   Ah.

**Maid**   That's why the cook quit.

**Anna**   Is it?

**Claire**   . . . didn't like the entertainment?

**Maid**   No, I tell a lie. I'd put th' tray *down*, do you see, but I wz holdin' *on* to it, on to the handles, like, while it was on the counter.

**Claire**   . . . thank you, yes.

**Maid**   . . . for

**Claire**   . . . that's quite enough.

**Maid**   For 'balance'. (*Pause.*)

**Claire**   Ah, yes.

**Maid**   And I'm afraid I've spilt the milk. (**Maid** *cries.*)

**Anna**   Oh, Man – oh, Adversary Implacable. What does one not sacrifice upon the altar of your merciless caprice? (*To* **Maid**.) Go away. You're fired.

**Claire**   Are you deaf? You're sacked. Go away now, go home.

**Maid**   I can't go home.

**Anna**   Can't you see, we have troubles of our own?

**Claire**   Have you no sympathy?

**Maid**   I can't go home, I'm *ruined*.

**Claire**   You ain't ruined. Just don't *tell* nobody. You dense *cow*. Don't tell anyone. And pray to the gods your friend hasn't given you the pox. Or a child. (**Maid** *cries*.) Shall I write it *down* for you . . . ?

**Anna**   Go, go, go, go away, you sad, immoral harlot.

**Maid**   I don't know what to *do*.

**Claire**   Well, what would your Auld Granny say?

**Maid**   I don't know.

**Claire**   Well, go home and ask her.

**Maid**   She's dead.

**Claire**   She should have taken better care of herself.

**Maid**   Waal, she lived a long life.

**Claire**   Oh, good.

**Maid**   She was forty.

**Anna**   . . . Ah ha . . .

**Maid**   But she always said, My Gran, she would Reach Out from Beyond the Grave.

**Claire**   Told Fortunes, did she?

**Anna**   Go away.

**Claire**   Turned the odd trick? Fill up the Family Larder?

**Maid**   . . . she had the second sight.

**Claire**   . . . how handy.

**Maid**   The islanders said she could see right through a man and two yards into the dirt that he stood on. One time, Annie MacPherson lost her locket. Actually, she lost it more than once. She never could hold on to anything. She used to tie her shovel to her apron strings when she went out to work in the garden. That's how she broke her ankle. One time, she baked a trowel in a pie. (*Pause.*) I must pull up me bootstraps. Yer right. I'll go.

**Claire**    Oh top *hole*! (*Pause.*)

**Anna**    Happy Day.

**Maid**    Because Me Auld Gran used to say . . .

**Claire**    Oh, for Christ's sake, let her void herself.

**Anna**    What did your Auld Gran say?

**Maid**    'Life is Froth and Life is Bubble. Two things stand like stone. Kindness in another's trouble. Courage in your own.' (*Pause.*)

**Maid** *exits.*

**Claire**    We've fallen victim to the worst sin.

**Anna**    Farting in Church?

**Claire**    Despair.

**Anna**    . . . that is the worst sin?

**Claire**    The girl is right.

**Anna**    In what particular?

**Claire**    Fine. We are mired in difficulties. We must extricate ourselves.

**Anna**    I am all attention.

**Claire**    Our fortunes are turned upon the unwonted discovery in your home of a specific emerald necklace.

**Anna**    In brief.

**Claire**    All, then, we must do is excuse its presence here.

**Anna**    You bound before me.

**Claire**    Look here: You are a jeweler. You are a lapidary. He brought the Emerald to you to have it Reset. (*Pause.*)

**Anna**    No.

**Claire**  You are a sleuth. You are a detectress.
Commissioned to locate and restore the stolen necklace.

**Anna**  . . . Mmm . . .

**Claire**  You are a valuer for an Assurance Firm.

**Anna**  Hold *hard*. Hold *hard*. . . . No no no no better than
that. Better than that *far:* do you see? You brought her to
me. You brought the little twat here. You brought the
trollop here to . . .

**Maid** *enters. Pause.*

**Anna**  What?

**Maid**  Are ye angry with me, mum?

**Anna**  Do you know why you people perished? Do you
know? In your precious potato famine? Do you think it was
chance? You *died*, through a criminal lack of concern for the
nitrogen content of the soil. (*Pause.*)

**Maid** *exits crying.*

**Claire**  Where were we?

**Anna**  . . . it is gone.

**Claire**  No, I deny it.

**Anna**  It is vanished.

**Claire**  *Best* of friends. Most inventive of Preceptors . . .

**Anna**  You brought her here . . . (*Pause.*) No.

**Claire**  How may I retrieve that Philosopher's stone,
which bid fair to repair our fortunes? How can I jog your
memory?

**Anna**  No, it is gone.

**Claire**  How may I recruit your dispersed fancies?

**Anna**  Distract me.

**Claire**    Uh, uh, uh . . . Once two children went into the woods . . .

**Anna**    No.

**Claire**    All right, Once upon a time . . . Once in the course of human events, wait: Awake!
    The roseate hue of dawn steals o'er the sleeping copse.
    Hark! Hark! The hunting horn . . . something . . .
        something . . .
    'Foxes' . . .

**Anna**    Yes. Yes. I have it.

**Claire**    '. . . Little kit fox, why weep'st thou? For, though your daddy dies, he offers healthy amusement to the county' . . . Uh . . .

**Anna**    Have you run down?

**Claire**    I seem to.

**Anna**    Good. I have the Perfect Plan.

**Claire**    I beg your pardon – Disgorge it.

**Anna**    Upon the one proviso.

**Claire**    . . . a proviso?

**Anna**    That should I resurrect our Fortunes, you swear to see this twit no more.

**Claire**    You swine.

**Anna**    Everything has a price.

**Claire**    You Visigoth.

**Anna**    And having a price, has a price tag, read it.

**Claire**    I shall see her the once.

**Anna**    Granted.

**Claire**    In privacy.

**Anna**    For how long?

**Claire**   An afternoon.

**Anna**   Done.

**Claire**   You concede so blithely. Why?

**Anna**   And she unbroken to the Bit? All innocent of the Chafe of the Saddle . . . And Shy of the Touch of Man. Progress how you will, I feel the one afternoon will hardly avail you.

**Claire**   That will be as it may.

**Anna**   And I want to watch.

**Claire**   Outside of the room.

**Anna**   I'll fetch the auger.

**Claire**   Tell me the plan.

**Anna**   You tell the girl that her father came, to visit a Famous Clairvoyant . . .

**Claire**   Mmm.

**Anna**   Madame de . . .

**Claire**   No, I get ya . . .

**Anna**   And he brought her mother's Jewel . . .

**Claire**   Say on . . .

**Anna**   In order to divine by it. (*Pause.*) Whdja Think?

**Claire**   It is the least credible explanation of Human Behavior I have ever heard.

**Anna**   Of course. But you miss the point.

**Claire**   The point being . . .

**Anna**   That it is not to be *believed* . . .

**Claire**   Mmm?

**Anna**   Our tale is offered, but as a fig leaf of propriety. Not to 'explain', but to clothe with the, the . . .

**Claire**    Mantle of decency.

**Anna**    Yes. That behavior it would be irksome to hear explained.

**Claire**    You are a Medium.

**Anna**    Yes.

**Claire**    And her *Father* . . .

**Anna**    Yes.

**Claire**    He heard, while abroad . . .

**Anna**    Yes.

**Claire**    Heard, yes, while in the Orient. Of a Fortune-Teller.

**Anna**    Mmm.

**Maid** *enters.*

**Maid**    I've come to get me wages.

**Claire**    One moment, a seer, who could conjure . . .

**Anna**    By means of the Jewel.

**Claire**    Now, there you've lost me.

**Anna**    You take the jewel and gaze into it, as into a crystal ball, to determine, do you see? Both the woman's secret ills, and their alleviation.

**Claire**    . . . the woman.

**Anna**    Yes.

**Claire**    What woman?

**Anna**    Her mother.

**Claire**    Whose mother?

**Anna**    Your friend's mother. My protector's wife. You see, we tell her that's why her father *came.* Not to *betray* his wife, no, no, no, but to *aid* her. What *is* her problem, by the way? Has your friend spoken of it?

**Claire**    The Mother?

**Anna**    Yes.

**Claire**    She is subject, it seems, to those unnamed vagrant . . . How did you know she *has* a problem?

**Anna**    Her husband has been in the Orient for Seven Years.

**Claire**    As long as that.

**Anna**    He tells me.

**Claire**    And she lacked the, the . . .

**Anna**    Let us say the capacity for independent *action*.

**Claire** (*pause*)    Makes you think . . .

**Anna**    Well, I'd hardly go *that* far.

**Maid**    I've come to get me wages.

**Claire**    And so, . . .

**Anna**    So the Husband, do you see, out of Concern.

**Claire**    Concern, yes.

**Anna**    On his return from Abroad, brought in his wife's jewel, to allow the medium . . .

**Claire**    Mmm.

**Anna**    . . . to Divine with it. (*Pause.*)

**Claire**    Fine. Which leaves only this. How does one explain to the father his daughter's exceptional presence here?

**Anna**    Oh, faugh.

**Claire**    Ah. Tis not your ox was gored. Where is your Bible *now*?

**Anna**    It's in the morning room.

**Maid**    I've come to get me wages.

**Claire**    All right, then, can you think that your protector will continue in his liaison with one *whose Best Friend* had debauched his little girl?

**Anna**    Do you suggest he might object?

**Claire**    You must get out more.

**Anna**    *Truly? (Pause.)*

**Claire**    Yes.

**Anna**    What has become of liberality? Of Progressive thought? Of . . .

**Claire**    Gone at the slightest hint of difficulty.

**Anna**    My oh my.

**Claire**    Disappeared like an Oil Stock newly invested in by a young Widow.

**Anna**    . . . I ask you.

**Claire**    . . . like a tarsier, at the hint of False Dawn.

**Anna**    What is a tarsier?

**Claire**    It is an East Indian Rodent.

**Anna**    *Is* it?

**Claire**    I believe it is.

**Anna**    Noteworthy for its skittishness?

**Claire**    It is proverbial . . . but.

**Anna**    . . . live and learn.

**Claire**    How do we explain to the father the presence here of his little girl?

**Anna**    We tell him the selfsame thing.

**Claire**   To wit:

**Anna**   She came here to consult a fortune-teller.

**Claire**   But he knows you're not a fortune-teller.

**Anna**   We tell him *you*'re the fortune-teller.

**Claire**   I'm a fortune-teller, too?

**Anna**   Mmm.

**Claire**   Does that mean I, too, must wear a funny hat?

**Anna**   If necessary. (*Pause.*)

**Claire**   But could such a Byzantine rodomontade restore
the girl to me? Could it convince the father?

**Anna**   Men live but to be deceived.

**Claire**   They do?

**Anna**   Well, what have I done but deceive him? My
protector loves me. He requires my *aid*. How to continue
with me when all the world conspires to the contrary. We
will mint for him his excuse. And our poor simpering effort
will, once again, conquer all. (*Pause.*)

**Claire**   I have underestimated you.

**Anna**   I'm quite aware of it. Oh, my word, in fine: we shall
have a *séance*. Eh? Eh?

**Claire**   A Séance.

**Anna**   At Which Séance, I, Madame de . . .

**Claire**   Mmm.

**Maid**   Miss . . .

**Anna**   Yes, shut up one moment, will you . . . ? Will put
all . . .

**Maid**   Miss . . .

**Anna**   Will put all aright.

**Claire**    A Séance.

**Anna**    At which:

**Claire**    At which, amidst both the Mumbo and the Jumbo . . .

**Anna**    Mmm.

**Claire**    You divine . . .

**Anna**    Yes.

**Claire**    By means of the Jewel . . .

**Anna** (*pause*)    But what do we know, what can we adduce or invent of the clairvoyant?

**Maid**    Miss . . .

**Claire**    Shut up for a moment, will you?

**Maid**    It's a monkey.

**Claire**    How, at this séance, shall we convince each, of our aforementioned supernormal powers?

**Anna**    We shall present them with, with circumstantial facts of their previous lives. (*Pause.*)

**Claire**    The man was seven years in India.

**Anna**    What do we know of India . . . ? (*Pause.*)

**Claire**    Ah, well . . .

**Anna**    *How* I wish I read . . .

**Claire**    *India* . . . (*Pause.*)

**Anna**    . . . the, the, the . . .

**Claire**    *'India'* . . .

**Anna**    India is possessed of . . . Or, at the risk of *Pedantry*:

**Claire**    Please.

**Anna**    India is Bounded on the North by . . .

**Maid**   It's a monkey.

**Claire**   Have you not, lacking sufficient awe, that sense of fitness to stand mute before your betters?

**Maid**   Mum?

**Claire**   Go away or we shall have a policeman in to shoot you and stick your head on a pike.

**Maid**   Begging your pardon. It's a monkey.

**Anna**   What's a monkey?

**Maid**   A tarsier. My Dad had one in Bengal.

**Claire**   In Bengal?

**Maid**   Yuh.

**Anna**   Bengal. In India.

**Maid**   That's right.

**Anna**   And did he, as one would assume, regale you with tales of that dark, unknowable land?

**Maid**   Yes, miss.

**Anna** (*to* **Claire**)   Write to invite them to our séance.

**Claire**   . . . but, but, how . . .

**Anna**   We shall deluge them with, folk, folk wisdom.

**Claire**   Folk wisdom . . . ?

**Anna**   Women's Wisdom, do you see? The Sayings of the Auld Grandmarm.

**Claire**   The trash the slavey's grandma gibbered.

**Anna**   Let it *extract* us from our difficulties. I shall adopt it as that axiom which rules my life. *Molly:*

**Maid**   I suppose it's bootless to beg for a character.

**Anna**   I . . .

**Maid**   Just give me me wages.

**Anna**   Molly, Dear . . . ?

**Maid**   Did ye want to count the Silver?

**Anna**   How *Colorful* . . .!

**Maid**   For I've got to look out for meself, you know, for when you turn on me.

**Anna**   As if we could distrust you! How I *love* that Earthy Humor.

**Claire**   Earthy Humor, yes.

**Anna**   So . . .

**Claire**   Close to the soil. Your mistress would opine perhaps she's been too hasty.

**Maid**   Too hasty . . .

**Anna**   Yes. I . . .

**Claire**   She withdraws the Edict . . .

**Maid**   The edict.

**Claire**   The, the Ukase . . . the . . .

**Anna**   I take back what I said.

**Claire**   And she *hopes*. That you will see fit to remain in . . .

**Anna**   In my *Service*.

*Pause.*

**Maid**   Yeh want me to stay.

**Claire**   We want you to help us plan a sort of party.

**Maid**   Waal, I don't know.

**Anna**   What don't you know?

**Maid**   . . . after th' things you've said . . .

**Claire**   Oh, bullshit. Sit down, or we'll throw you in the streets to starve, pox-ridden and pregnant.

**Anna**   Nora, oblige us. Please tell us about your grandmother.

**Maid**   Yes, mum.

**Anna**   You see? You see how it profits? One must keep a civil tongue in one's mouth.

**Claire**   Mmm.

**Anna**   . . . it need not be one's own.

**Claire**   Well – ain't *you* wicked . . .


## Scene Two

**Anna** *and* **Claire** *in vaguely Middle Eastern garb.* **Claire** *goes to examine herself in a mirror.*

**Claire**   The couture of the paranormal does not well withstand the gaze of day.

**Anna**   Like that of the boudoir.

**Claire**   Pray do not taunt me.

**Anna**   Quite right. (*Pause.*)

**Claire**   I feel I'd like to climb beneath some lavishly appointed rock.

**Anna**   It is the waiting galls one.

**Claire**   Is it?

**Anna**   Ah, yes, we suffer for our sins, we suffer for them.

**Claire**   But not before we have made *others* suffer for them.

**Anna**   You still indict me for our dilemma?

**Claire**  I find myself hoping to lure back my love with a funny hat.

**Anna**  Is that not a woman's lot?

**Claire**  How ill philosophy becomes you.

**Anna**  They will respond.

**Claire**  I cannot think so. Oh, I am other than well.

**Anna**  Do you know I have noticed. In the midst of this or that upheaval, that at times, the spirit is relieved by the simple increase of *bulk* in the diet. (*Pause.*)

**Claire**  What *is* bulk?

**Anna**  *Bulk*, and I ask your pardon in advance,

**Claire**  . . . please.

**Anna**  is that which tends toward the cleansing of, I believe, the *colon*, or whatever the . . . the . . . (*Pause.*)

**Claire**  . . . I never could abide 'learning', do you know . . .

**Anna**  Mmm.

**Claire**  . . . always seemed so 'pushy'.

**Anna**  Yes. Down through the ages, it is one of the historic tools of the Social Climber.

**Claire**  Are my seams straight?

**Anna**  Euclidean.

*The* **Maid** *enters. All stand.*

**Anna**  Is the room prepared?

**Maid**  All prepared, mum . . .

**Anna**  Report.

**Maid**   We got the draperies drawn, the table moved, the chairs all thronged together so the people's knees will touch . . .

**Anna**   The candles . . . ?

**Maid**   I've lit 'em.

**Anna**   Did you not say . . . did you not say . . . We must wait till the incantation?

**Claire**   Isn't that what your Auld Gran Said?

**Anna**   . . . were we not *told* . . . we must *wait* till the *incantation* . . .

**Claire**   Why have you lit the candles?

**Maid**   Well, the sun's goin' down. (*Pause.*) Where's your guests?

**Anna**   Withdraw until you're called.

**Maid** *exits.*

**Claire**   They will not come. They will not respond. We shall be left two foolish old women, trusting to chemistry and candlelight. (*Pause.*)

**Anna**   Be strong.

**Claire**   Easy for you.

**Anna**   If my protector withdraws his support, I am reduced to poverty, but do you see me complain?

**Claire**   I could compass the girl's waist with my two small hands. But perhaps I grow too technical.

**Anna**   Oh God oh God oh God of hosts, how we are Reduced . . . how the Shadow of Poverty . . . How *Stress* . . .

**Claire**   What is Of Hosts?

**Anna**   It connotes 'of Many'.

**Claire**   How *cunning* of it . . .

**Anna**    Why do you dismiss the comfort of such sacred and archaic language?

**Claire**    I was brought up in a barn.

**Maid** *reenters.*

**Anna** (*to* **Maid**)    What?

**Maid**    I'm worried, mum.

**Anna**    No need to worry. For men live to be deceived. They would rather be deceived than sated.

**Maid**    No, that ain't what worries me.

**Claire**    What worries you?

**Maid**    What if I have a child?

**Claire**    One waits until the colder months, and exposes them in a tree.

**Anna**    Off you go! (**Maid** *exits. Pause.*) May I ask you, do you never feel that you've missed something?

**Claire**    What would that be?

**Anna**    Motherhood.

**Claire**    Were I to say that the joys of conception, parturition and lactation had been vouchsafed to me I would tell a lie.

**Anna**    Yes. But certain women profit from it.

**Claire**    In what way?

**Anna**    They, they have *children.*

**Claire**    Apart from that.

**Anna**    No. I take your point.

**Maid** (*reentering*)    We ain't got no new candles. (*Pause.*)

**Claire**    Isn't this always the way.

**Anna**    Run quick and get them. Hurry. Go.

**Maid** *exits.*

**Claire**    They have abandoned us. What time is it? They will not come.

**Anna**    They will come.

**Claire**    What will make them come?

**Anna**    We shall dispatch a second note.

**Claire**    A second note?

**Anna** (*to* **Maid**, *calling after her*)    Send for a messenger.

**Claire**    And how will this second note be more effective than the first?

**Anna**    WE SHALL INVITE THE WIFE!

**Claire**    . . . the wife . . . ?

**Anna**    How blind I have been. *If* we are soothsayers. As we are. *If* we possess the power to alleviate pain, to, to cure her vapors, to . . .

**Claire**    . . . yes . . . ?

**Anna**    Then let us *cure* the *wife*! The wife is the cornerstone! With her endorsement, both the man and the girl are licensed to frequent our home. How *blind* I have been. (*She writes.*) 'Madame de blah blah, to whom the future and the past are one, awaits to set your mind at rest. Having divined and prognosticated by the means of *your jewel* . . .' Ha ha ha ha ha. 'And having, at length, diagnosed the cause of your discomfort, she invites you.'

**Claire**    She will not come.

**Anna**    She *will* come, and let her call it 'Doubt' or 'Indignation', let her call it what she will, she must succumb to her curiosity . . . It is the weakness of the sex. (*Doorbell.* **Maid** *passes through.*) Who is it?

**Maid**    A messenger.

**Anna**   . . . arrived so soon? Bid him attend a moment . . . 'And to perfect, for you, through the accumulation and dispersal of tea leaves, the lessons of the crystal ball, and the application of exotic herbs.' (Resist *that* if you can. She cannot. For women are . . .)

**Claire**   . . . pray do not say what we are. I know too well what we are . . .

**Anna**   Then you know the wife must come. I've sussed out her fulcrum, it is *Curiosity*, and we have her on the hip. I bet you a new Hat. (*Continues writing.*) 'et *cetera*, to remove those noxious ethereal influences we have found surround you. And restore your spirits and your soul. In the name of various gods, I remain . . .'

**Maid** *reenters with a letter.* **Anna** *hands the* **Maid** *the note.*

**Anna**   Give the messenger this. Thank him for his prompt response.

**Maid**   For what response?

**Anna**   To our summons.

**Maid**   What summons, mum?

**Anna**   We summoned him to take a letter.

**Maid**   No, mum. He *brought* a letter. (*Pause.*) He *brought* a letter. (*Exits.*)

**Claire** *takes the letter. Opens it.*

**Claire** (*reads*)   Who is Rehab the Harlot?

**Anna**   I believe it is for me.

**Claire**   Will you hear your fate?

**Anna**   I am prepared. (*Reads.*) It is from his attorney. They have decamped. The entire family. He will . . . he has, yes, he has terminated the, the 'consultation fees', which, of late, it has been his use to pay me.

**Claire**   . . . he no longer desires to consult with you . . .

**Anna**    . . . and he requires the immediate return of his wife's necklace, which had somehow found its accidental way into my possession.

**Claire**    . . . he wants his sparkler back . . .

**Anna**    . . . absent which . . . legal remedies, criminal proceedings, bailiff, theft . . . jail . . .

**Claire**    Oh, dear.

**Anna**    . . . and he will send an emissary to collect the Jewel.

**Claire** (*takes the letter*)    And pop goes the entire weasel. (*Pause.*)

**Anna**    I fear I was mistaken in his steadfastness. (*Pause.*)

**Claire**    You must keep it, of course.

**Anna**    Keep?

**Claire**    The Jewel.

**Anna**    The Jewel. I cannot.

**Claire**    You Must.

**Anna**    How can I?

**Claire**    He gave it to you.

**Anna**    It was not his to give.

**Claire**    Are all our possessions, and all our joys, but loaned on *sufferance*, and subject to the whim of men? He's broke his promise. He's deceived you. He's had the use of your body, and he paid for it with stolen goods. For God's sake keep the necklace.

**Anna**    You are *distraught.*

**Claire**    Have I not cause?

**Maid** (*reentering*)    I'm goin' for the candles, mum.

**Anna**    What?

**Maid**   I'm goin' for th' . . .

**Claire**   I don't think we'll require them. (*Pause.*) I doubt that we could pay for them.

**Maid** *exits.*

**Anna**   Well, are we worse off than we were before?

**Claire**   What a dreary standard by which to gauge one's life.

**Anna**   What choice have we but to take heart?

**Claire**   Are you not, then, chilled by the spectre of poverty?

**Anna**   . . . by poverty?

**Claire**   Yes.

**Anna**   Doth not the Bible teach us to leave ungleaned the corners of our fields?

**Claire**   I have no idea.

**Anna**   I assure you.

**Claire**   And what might that mean?

**Anna**   That the urge, at the risk of tendentiousness . . .

**Claire**   . . . please.

**Anna**   To Consume All.

**Claire**   Yes *I* get ya . . .

**Anna**   Oh good. (*Pause.*) And, and . . .

**Claire**   . . . yes?

**Anna**   Might we not then deduce . . . then, that *true* happiness might lie . . . not in obtaining the, the object of one's . . .

**Claire**   . . . lust.

**Anna**   If you will, but, in being *free* of it? Would *that* not be joy? (*Pause.*)

**Claire**   No. (*Pause.*)

**Anna**   Oh.

**Claire**   But thank you for asking.

**Anna**   Look here: if we have enough to eat, suitably cut raiment, and shelter from the storm, what do we care?

**Claire**   You are too good.

**Anna**   Not at all. I'm merely practical.

**Claire**   I have lost her. And with her, the last good instant of my youth.

**Anna**   Oh, dear . . .

**Claire**   No, it all went pear-shaped.

**Anna**   What went all pear-shaped?

**Claire**   My life.

**Anna**   Your life, eh?

**Claire**   Which once shone so promising.

**Anna**   So many things are more amusing in Prospect, don't you find, than . . .

**Claire**   Than in Actuality?

**Anna**   Yes.

**Claire**   No, I do not.

**Anna**   Mmm.

**Claire**   But I treasure your intention to amuse me.

**Anna**   *Do* you?

**Claire**   Quite diverting.

**Maid** (*entering*)   Mum . . .

**Anna**  No, but may one not . . .

**Maid**  Mum.

**Anna**  One moment, Make that Leap, That, that Act of Renunciation which . . .

**Maid**  Mum.

**Anna**  . . . shut up. And, and may we not seek that, that . . .

**Maid**  Mum.

**Anna**  One moment, that, that State of Grace, that . . .

**Claire**  I don't think so . . .

**Anna**  Of, of *acceptance*, yes, if it is offered. Yes, and I think it *is* constantly . . .

**Maid**  Mum.

**Anna**  One moment. As at a Perfect Inn . . .

**Maid**  The cook said you could kiss her ass 'til Michaelmas . . .

**Anna**  . . . an Inn or hostel . . .

**Maid**  . . . I just remembered.

**Anna**  (*to exiting* **Maid**) . . . Thank you . . . Welcoming the legitimately weary.

**Claire**  . . . no.

**Anna**  Yes. Ministering to the travelers as they trod that way, do you see, they must trod in any case.

**Claire**  Yes. That would be no end of jolly. Oh, Age, Age, Dreadful Age.

**Anna**  As long as, as long as one has not 'done evil' . . . (*Pause.*)

**Claire**  . . . done evil?

**Anna**    Yes. Caused *pain*, or . . .

**Claire**    . . . and, indeed, I have gained nothing and have caused *you* pain.

**Anna**    Yes, some, perhaps, but . . .

**Claire**    *That* is a sin . . .

**Anna**    No, no, a *slip*, perhaps, done in exuberance. But not a true Error . . .

**Claire**    Then what would be example of true error?

**Anna**    . . . writing in purple *ink*, or . . .

**Claire**    . . . you are too good to live.

**Anna**    Is that so?

**Claire**    I regret that I have enmeshed you in my cabal of loss.

**Anna**    Oh pray, do not descend to the literary. (*Pause.*) *Are* we so badly off? Could we not strive to exist on my income?

**Claire**    Indeed, how . . . ?

**Anna**    Do they not say two can live as cheap as one?

**Claire**    No doubt. The world is full of fools and if one listens long enough, one may hear damn near anything.

**Anna**    But if we curtailed our expenditures, could we not sustain ourselves, say, in the country?

**Claire**    In the country! You, who, self-confessed, can neither hum nor fart. (*Pause.*) Hum nor fart. (*Pause.*) Fart nor hum. (*Pause.*)

**Anna**    'Farm nor hunt'?

**Claire**    Precisely. What would we do in the country? Sit and pray for dissolution. Like goldfish. Fit only to sicken and die. (*Pause.*)

**Anna**    . . . I *can* hum, you know.

**Claire**    Can you indeed?

**Anna**    I could *always* hum. I could not *'whistle'*. This is not the first time you've confused them. How affective are the very foibles of those we love? I think that it is charming. What do you think? (*Pause.*) Is it charming?

**Claire**    It is charming if you are charmed by it. (*Pause.*)

**Anna**    Why do you reject those niceties of speech and conduct nature has contrived to even our rough ways?

**Claire**    I have ruint what I touched.

**Anna**    . . . Claire . . .

**Claire**    Perhaps, as has no doubt been observed before, we human beings are but a plague upon the rocks or plants . . . and perhaps I am small potatoes. Perhaps I am not potatoes at all.

**Anna**    Oh, my dear, you must have loved her.

**Claire**    I *do* love her.

**Anna**    Well. You, you will have her In Retrospect.

**Claire**    In retrospect?

**Anna**    As, do you see, as the vision of a flame. Which persists. After the flame is gone.

**Claire**    No, I don't get you.

**Anna**    When you blow the candle out.

**Claire**    The flame lasts?

**Anna**    The vision. The *vision* of the flame.

**Claire**    . . . oh, God, . . . no. Do not look on me. Time drags on. And each day I spin Gold into flax.

**Anna**    My dear, could we not intuit, in this Reversal, the, the operations of a Greater Hand?

**Claire**    A Greater Hand?

**Anna**   A Brake, or Governor, upon . . .

**Claire**   A 'brake' . . .

**Anna**   Both our, I believe it, Happiness and Folly.

**Claire**   If I could but believe . . .

**Anna**   But the point is not to believe but to decide.

**Claire**   Oh, my dear. You always were too good for me. God bless you in your naiveté. And when you reminisce, forgive me.

**Anna**   When I reminisce . . . ? (*Pause.*)

**Claire**   You understand that my presence here would be a drain upon both your emotions and your treasury. (*Pause.*) I have spoiled your establishment and traduced your affections. Better for us both to part.

**Anna** (*pause*)   Oh.

**Claire**   I know you understand.

**Anna**   And I cannot dissuade you?

**Claire**   I fear you cannot.

**Anna** (*pause*)   But . . .

**Claire**   Bless you. Your efforts would be in vain.

**Anna**   You once said, you could be happy alone with me in a Garret.

**Claire**   And once I could. Forgive me.

**Anna** (*pause*)   I will fetch the Jewel. (*Exits.*)

**Maid** *enters.*

**Claire**   All undone by Men.

**Maid**   Excuse me, mum.

**Claire**   Undone by Men, I opined. Are you deaf?

**Maid**   What, mum?

**Claire**    I made fair to make common cause with you, do you see? You, ravaged and abandoned. Myself done out of my birthright. By Men. (*To* **Maid**.) Where are you rushing to?

**Maid**    I'm goin' for the candles, mum.

**Claire**    We don't require them now, do you see? For our schemes have miscarried. (*Pause.*) How odd to've supposed a possible alternative.

**Maid**    I beg your pardon, mum.

**Claire**    I said we don't require the candles. (*Pause.*) What?

**Maid**    I tell a lie.

**Claire**    Again?

**Maid**    Yes, mum. An' I must beg your pardon.

**Claire**    What was the lie?

**Maid**    I'm goin' to see me fella.

**Claire**    See yer fellow, is it?

**Maid**    Yes, mum.

**Claire**    I thought he'd abandoned you.

**Maid**    No, mum. He changed his mind.

**Claire**    Oh, good.

**Maid**    He just sent word as how he wants to meet me in the park to 'discuss' something.

**Claire**    Whatever would *that* be? Some tender of his 'troth', so on?

**Maid**    I hope so, mum.

**Claire**    Then of course. Off you go. (**Maid** *exits.*) Off you go to your Bower of Bliss. Off you go to your sweet narcotic. Two souls resubsumed in oblivion. Off you go. I will stay here. (*Pause.*)

**Anna** *enters.*

**Anna**   Where is the Slavey?

**Claire**   Gone out.

**Anna**   When?

**Claire**   Just now.

**Anna**   I have been robbed.

**Claire**   What can you mean?

**Anna**   The jewel is gone.

**Claire**   Where did you look?

**Anna**   Everywhere.

**Claire**   It cannot be.

**Anna**   It is.

**Claire**   Infamia.

**Anna**   They have destroyed me.

**Claire**   The girl took the Jewel?

**Anna**   She, it must be, and her accomplice.

**Claire**   'That man.'

**Anna**   Help me.

**Claire**   Lord, what is not fleeing, here below?

**Anna**   They shall cart me to jail.

**Claire**   . . . Anna . . .

**Anna**   What shall I do? I cannot bear rebuke, let alone
*incarceration* . . . They will come with, what are they called?
One wears them on one's wrists.

**Claire**   Manacles.

**Anna**   And take me away. I, who have required from life
so little . . .

**Claire**  My dear . . .

**Anna**  And now, and now . . .

**Claire**  We can prevail upon your protector.

**Anna**  He has denounced me and decamped.

**Claire**  The cad.

**Anna**  And hidden in That woman's skirts. His wife.

**Claire**  What craven cowards they are.

**Anna**  But, as they are, always in possession of the Field, how would they learn Nobility?

**Claire**  But would he, in *truth*, consign you to jail?

**Anna**  Oh, my dear, undoubtedly. He has so much of which he is ashamed.

**Claire**  As do I.

**Anna**  Please?

**Claire**  I am cause of your misfortune. If I had not brought the child here, does not such a speech occur to you?

**Anna**  But: None of us is perfect. Each is not only permitted but required to repent . . . And if to repent, then of necessity, to err. It is now my lot to attempt that most profoundly difficult of human tasks.

**Claire**  To forgive one who has wronged you?

**Anna**  No, to pack when rushed. What shall I want in a cell? It is so hard to think on the instant. I'll take your portrait. (*Starts to exit.*)

**Claire**  Take my portrait?

**Anna**  The one in the brown kerseymere. You remember.

**Claire**  I thought he'd got the nose wrong.

**Anna**  How little you know of yourself. (*Starts, again, to exit.*)

**Claire**   Oh, for God's sake: pack for two.

**Anna**   . . . I'm sorry?

**Claire**   I shall, of course, accompany you.

**Anna**   No.

**Claire**   To the contrary.

**Anna**   A touch *Ancien Régime*, don't you think?

**Claire**   I profoundly hope so.

**Anna**   But you could not abide Jail.

**Claire**   What have I to fear?

**Anna**   The food, the clothing and the conversation.

**Claire**   We shall brave them together.

**Anna**   Shall we?

**Claire**   Every circumstance conspires to so instruct me.

**Anna**   And do you not find such instruction onerous?

**Claire**   I do not.

**Anna**   How can I thank you?

**Claire**   Hear my confession.

**Anna**   Speak to me.

**Claire**   I abhor chintz. (*Pause.*)

**Anna**   You said that you liked it.

**Claire**   I spoke in jest.

**Anna**   Yes, perhaps I have wronged you, too.

*Doorbell.*

**Anna**   That would be the bailiff.

**Claire**   Are you prepared?

**Anna**   I'll have the girl fetch my wrap.

**Claire**    The girl is gone.

**Anna**    Then I shall fetch my wrap myself.

**Claire**    Oh God, so it begins.

**Anna** *exits.*

**Claire**    This, then, would be 'one of the things which are too bad'. But if she can bravely say 'so be it', how can I but emulate her? Oh! I achieved enlightenment! Enter then, sir, and do your worst.

**Maid** *enters. Pause.*

**Claire**    Vandal, how dare you return?

**Maid**    I brought a . . .

**Claire**    How do you find the gall?

**Maid**    I brought . . .

**Claire**    You brought, what? A fell request for *Ransom*?

**Maid**    Miss?

**Claire**    What business have you here?

**Maid**    I thought I'd make the tea. (*Pause.*)

**Claire**    The Tea?

**Maid**    It's teatime.

**Claire**    Where is your mistress's necklace?

**Maid**    In the Bible.

**Claire**    . . . in the Bible?

**Maid**    In the morning room. She left it in there, marking her place.

**Claire**    Did she, indeed?

**Maid**    She did. She never can remember where she put it.

**Claire**    . . . yes. (*Pause.*)

**Maid**   I brought you a note.

**Claire**   A Note.

**Maid**   There's a young lady, gave it to me.

**Claire**   A young lady?

**Maid**   In a conveyance, waitin' on the corner.

**Claire**   Give me the note.

**Maid** *hands her the note.* **Claire** *opens it and reads.*

**Maid**   She said she ain't got but the one instant she could stay, for yer answer. Though, I must say, she didn't have to be so *snappish*. For, din't I give up me meeting with me feller, just to bring the note in. D'you think she might let me step out this evening, do you think?

**Claire**   . . . step out?

**Maid**   Me mistress, as I had t'forgo me afternoon outing.

**Claire**   Developing a taste for the Carnal, are we?

**Maid**   Yes, miss. That's the sad part. Can't help meself.

**Claire**   Mmm.

**Maid**   D'you think she would? Let me step out this evening?

**Claire**   If you *do*, remember to instruct your friend to brush your back off when you get up from ground.

**Maid**   We do it up against a tree.

**Claire**   Isn't that hard on the legs?

**Maid**   Perhaps. But the view is better.

**Claire**   What in life is not a compromise.

**Maid**   Love. (*Pause.*)

**Claire**   May you find it so.

**Maid**   The girl can stay just the one minute, and then she'll be gone. (*Pause.*)

**Claire**   Just the one moment, and then she'll be gone.

**Maid**   You'll want me to take out your answer?

**Claire** *stops reading the note.*

**Claire**   No, there is no answer.

**Maid**   Very good, miss. Then I'll make the tea.

**Maid** *exits.* **Claire** *tears the note in half.*

**Anna** *reenters, carrying a small carpetbag and portrait.*

**Claire**   You take so little.

**Anna**   I have what I require. Shall we await them in the air?

**Claire**   Await them . . . ?

**Anna**   Yes, the bailiffs.

**Claire**   . . . ah.

**Anna**   For it seems I am finished with this house.

**Claire**   Yes. Let us sit in the park, for I have various things I'd like to say to you.

**Anna**   But are you *resigned*? Are you, indeed, resigned to accompany me into Exile?

**Claire**   Not resigned, but honored.

**Anna**   Better than the best of friends.

**Claire**   And you shall be my preceptor.

**Anna**   . . . my dear? . . .

**Claire**   The world you see is not cruel. It possesses neither falsity nor guile. And it shall be my mission to protect you from it.

**Anna**   Then you are returned to me.

**Claire**   With all my heart.

**Anna**   But will your feelings never change?

**Claire**   That is not within my gift. But I will never leave you. Will that do?

**Anna**   I am content.

*Pause.* **Claire** *exits. The* **Maid** *enters.*

**Anna**   Mary: A gentleman will call for the Jewel.

**Maid**   Yes, mum.

**Anna**   It's in the Bible in the morning room. Give it to him.

**Maid**   Yes, mum.

**Anna**   And get a receipt.

**Anna** *starts to exit.* **Maid** *curtseys.* **Maid** *holds up a muff.*

**Maid**   Miss, your friend's forgot her muff.

**Anna** (*exiting*)   No – nothing in life is certain. That remains to be seen. (*Exits.*)

*Curtain.*

Lightning Source UK Ltd.
Milton Keynes UK
09 October 2009
144741UK00001B/30/A